The PETER POTENTIAL

DISCOVER THE LIFE YOU WERE MEANT TO LIVE

DAVID BUTLER   EMILY BELLE FREEMAN

ENSIGN
PEAK

Visit us at EnsignPeakPublishing.com

Library of Congress Cataloging-in-Publication Data
CIP data on file.
ISBN 978-1-60907-883-6

Printed in Canada
Friesens Corporation, Altona, Manitoba, Canada

10   9   8   7   6   5   4   3   2   1

For Steven,
who is bold
and has much good to offer

and

For Pom Pom,
whose gentle heart
overflows with devotion
1928–2014

PREFACE

Have you ever wondered how such an insignificant man as Peter became so remarkable?

The Bible is clear on this point: Peter saw himself as a simple fisherman—but the Lord saw him as a fisher of men, a leader among men, the one in whose hands He would place the keys of His kingdom. Jesus extended invitations to help Peter grow, change, and become prepared for the life he was meant to live.

This process of discovery is recorded in the Gospels. Although the journey took place over three years, with many invitations—some of which probably aren't even recorded in history—a few events seemed to be particularly significant to the process.

How do we know?

Have you ever noticed that some stories are repeated in the scriptures? Consider the loaves and the fishes, the lowering of the nets on the right side, the two storms at sea. In each of these examples it seems the same lesson was taught twice, with almost the same wording both times.

Why the repetition?

It's almost as if the Lord is saying, *There is something here you need to understand; I will teach it twice in case you miss it the first time.* There is a consistent pattern in these repeating lessons: The lesson was taught first, then an invitation was given to act, and then the lesson was reinforced a second time. And these lessons have something else in common: First the lesson was taught to a large group, and then the second time the lesson was taught on a personal level. These personal experiences with the Lord were crucial to Peter's journey. Through the process of teaching and inviting, the Lord mentored Peter so that he could discover the greatness within.

This is the Peter Potential.

But it's not just about Peter.

The Lord sees greatness in you.

Every invitation you accept from Him will lead you closer to discovering what it is.

Has anyone ever told you that you are
EXTRAORDINARY?

That you are destined for
REMARKABLE
THINGS?

That there is a SPARK OF
GREATNESS in you?

They should have.

"We ask ourselves,

Who am I to be brilliant, gorgeous, talented, fabulous?

ACTUALLY, WHO ARE
YOU NOT TO BE?

You are a child of God.
Your playing small does not serve the world.

THERE IS NOTHING ENLIGHTENED
ABOUT SHRINKING. . . .

We are all meant to shine. . . . We were born to make manifest the glory of God that is within us. It's not just in some of us;

IT'S IN EVERYONE."

—MARIANNE WILLIAMSON

Sometimes that is hard to believe—because you live such a normal life. But there is One who knows what you are destined to achieve.

And what if that Someone had the power to help you discover the life you were meant to live?

Would you accept the invitation?

COME

He was a simple fisherman on the shores of Galilee, but on that morning,

SIMON PETER WAS EXTENDED AN INVITATION THAT WOULD CHANGE THE COURSE OF HIS LIFE.

After spending the whole night fishing he had absolutely nothing to show for his labor. Despite his exhaustion, his aching hands worked with the nets—washing and mending.

Where others would walk away after a long night's work leaving tangled nets hanging, it was his nature to leave nothing undone.

He was deliberate in his actions— thorough.

Peter lifted his gaze to the rising of the sun and felt the boat shift behind him. He glanced over his shoulder and watched the Lord finish stepping on board.

Smiling at Peter, He gestured at the huge crowd gathering on the shore and then humbly asked if he would

THRUST OUT
A LITTLE

from the land.

LUKE 5:3, KJV

A simple invitation

THRUST OUT
A LITTLE...

A REMINDER THAT SMALL ACTIONS
CAN LEAD TO GREAT THINGS.

Because he was still tending to his nets, the request wasn't too much of an inconvenience, so Peter pushed off shore. He wondered at the pressing crowd. Perhaps they recognized it just as he had—this man taught with invitations that inspired change.

Peter listened intently to the message from the man he had grown to admire. What started out as curiosity quickly turned to captivation.

Peter stacked his nets and turned his focus to the Lord.

Once He finished teaching, the Lord turned to Peter and extended the next invitation . . .

LAUNCH OUT
INTO THE DEEP.

LUKE 5:4, KJV

The Savior did not intend to take Peter on a surface journey.

He was about to reach into the depths of his heart.

HE WANTED THE DEPTHS OF HIS SOUL.

The miracles He intended to perform would not happen in shallow water.

To accept the invitation, Peter could no longer be content with where he was. It would require lifting the anchor.

Peter's first reaction was an expression of frustration. "We toiled all night and took nothing!"

LUKE 5:5, ESV

After a long night of fishing, the last thing Peter wanted to do was let down his clean and mended nets for another attempted catch.

WHAT GOOD WOULD COME OF IT THIS TIME?

He ran calloused fingers through his tangled hair and looked down at nets now stacked and folded.

It was bad timing, really.

INCONVENIENT.

Logic told him it would be a waste.

But at the Lord's word Peter lifted the anchor,
LAUNCHED OUT INTO THE DEEP,
and let down his net.

"When they had done so, they caught such a
large number of fish that their nets began to break.
So they signaled their partners in the other boat to
come and help them, and they came and filled both
boats so full that they began to sink."

LUKE 5:6−7, NIV

For almost an hour confusion reigned.

Peter shouted out instructions to make sure all the fish were gathered and then divided the load to make sure the ships could bear the weight.

At regular intervals his partners would stop and slap Peter on the back, congratulating him for his ingenuity and good fortune.

There was a moment, amidst the cacophony of it all, when Peter glanced over at the Lord. He knew the truth:

IT WAS BECAUSE HE HAD
ACCEPTED THE INVITATION.

THAT IS WHY THE BOATS
WERE SINKING WITH
blessings.

THAT IS WHY THE NETS
WERE BREAKING WITH
goodness.

WHEN WAS THE LAST TIME
YOU ACCEPTED
an invitation
FROM THE LORD?

An ecstatic Peter rowed back to shore.

Already crowds were gathering to see the great catch—quite possibly the greatest single catch of his lifetime. Without a doubt, this was the best day of his professional career. Peter smiled.

THIS TIME HE WOULDN'T MIND MENDING BROKEN NETS.

Peter's eyes moved from the bursting nets, to the gathering crowd, and then rested on the Lord who had been watching him intently through it all.

Little did he know that the Savior was preparing to extend one more invitation—this one even more inconvenient and difficult to accept than the one before.

LEAVE BEHIND
YOUR NETS
AND FOLLOW ME.

SEE MATTHEW 4:19–20

WHAT DID PETER DO?

WHAT WOULD
YOU
DO?

"*To each* there comes in their lifetime a special moment when they are figuratively tapped on the shoulder and offered the chance to do a very special thing, UNIQUE TO THEM and fitted to their talents. What a tragedy if that moment finds them unprepared or unqualified for that which could have been their finest hour."

—WINSTON CHURCHILL

Perhaps you have been tapped.

Maybe the Lord has extended the same invitation to you to leave something behind. Yours might not be a fishing net, but it will be just as difficult to walk away from.

They can be so entangling, nets—of every kind.

Are you everything you could be?

WHAT IS HOLDING YOU BACK?

Because Peter wanted what the Lord had to offer more than he wanted the things that held him back, he left his nets straightway and followed Him.

What if Peter believed that being the most successful fisherman on the Sea of Galilee *was* his greatest potential?

What if Peter had not straightway left his nets that day?

IMAGINE THE LIFE HE
WOULD HAVE MISSED OUT ON.

He would never have discovered what the Lord saw in him.

WILL YOU?

"And Jesus said unto them, Come ye after me, and I will make you to become fishers of men."

MARK 1:17, KJV

WHAT COULD

HE MAKE

YOU

TO BECOME?

Launch out into the deep
Leave behind your nets
Follow Him

It was the second stormy night recorded in the Gospels. Dark. Foreboding. Peter was in the midst of a storm-tossed sea, rowing with the other apostles against the waves. They had done this before, these same apostles fighting against the anger of the sea.

Peter remembered thinking on the first occasion that if he had to face a storm, these eleven were the men he would want to face it with. More than half of them were fishermen by trade—none were strangers to storms on the sea.

BUT THERE HAD BEEN SOMETHING DIFFERENT ABOUT THAT STORM.

A great tempest had blown.

Wave after wave had beaten into the ship, until it seemed as if it were constantly covered with water. Eventually the ship had become so full they feared that it would sink.

In all their years of fishing, the apostles had never faced a storm with this intensity. It seemed bent on destroying them.

WHERE WAS THE LORD?

In desperation they had awakened the Master, pleading, "Lord, save us!"

MATTHEW 8:25, NLT

The Lord HAD SPOKEN

OF LITTLE FAITH

AND THE

POWER OF DOUBT

AND THEN HE HAD COMMANDED

THE WATER TO STILL AND

THE SKIES TO CALM

AND THERE WAS PEACE.

Now Peter's thoughts returned to the storm at hand.

It was the fourth watch, the darkest part of the night, and what Peter wanted to be doing was sleeping soundly under a star-filled sky.

But such was not to be the case.

His shoulders ached from the constant strain of fighting to right the boat against the fury of the waves.

He clung to the oar that felt as if it would be ripped out of his clasp and struggled to remember the lesson from the last storm about putting aside doubt and fear.

In the midst of crashing waves and the fury of the wind, it was hard to grasp onto the faith the Lord had spoken of.

WHERE WAS THE LORD?

Peter lifted his eyes to the clouds, wondering how much longer the wrath would continue.

Then he focused again on the raging sea.

The fear he was supposed to have set aside gripped his heart as he saw a figure approaching the ship.

HOW WAS IT POSSIBLE?

The figure seemed to be walking on top of the swollen waves.

Before he could cry out, the figure spoke: "Take courage! It is I; be not afraid."
MATTHEW 14:27, NIV

The familiar voice brought instant relief, and Peter immediately responded, "Lord, if it be thou, bid me come unto thee on the water."
MATTHEW 14:28, KJV

This time the Savior's invitation was captured in one word:

COME

MATTHEW 14:29

WHAT DID PETER DO?

WHAT WOULD

YOU

DO?

In that moment, it was as if time stood still. The world around him was silenced, muted. Peter stood at the edge of the ship, eyes fixed on the Lord, who stood with a hand outstretched, waiting. Peter was learning that sometimes accepting the invitations from the Lord required action—*deliberate actions focused on Him.*

He took a deep breath and then climbed over the edge of the ship and stepped into the water.

"AND WHEN PETER WAS COME
DOWN OUT OF THE SHIP,
HE WALKED
ON THE WATER,
TO GO TO JESUS."

MATTHEW 14:29, KJV

PETER, A FISHERMAN,
WALKED ON WATER!

WHAT COULD
YOU DO
WITH THE LORD?

You probably know this isn't where the story ends. Surprisingly, Peter walking on water is not even the part of the story that captivates us. It is what happens next that we tend to focus on . . .

It was the wind that distracted Peter.

It tangled his hair and brought with it the reality of the situation. Brushing it back out of his eyes, he saw the storm-raged waves surging around him and heard friends yelling from behind.

WHAT WAS HE DOING?

He was a fisherman. Fishermen belonged in the boat. That was just the way it was—the way it had always been.

The wind whipped at his hair, pulled at his clothes, and angered the waves.

IT'S NOT HARD FOR A
little mustard seed
TO BE BLOWN AWAY BY A
POWERFUL GUST OF WIND.

The same applies to a little faith.
PETER BEGAN TO SINK.

Do you know what it is to *doubt?*

Have you ever felt *afraid?*

Unequal to the task, inexperienced, not good enough?

Destined to fail?

Are you familiar with the *great storms* of life?

Have you ever approached the Lord
soaking wet and windblown?

In the sinking moments of life, when you have wondered if you might drown, have you ever cried out,

"LORD, SAVE ME"?

MATTHEW 14:30, NIV

In those sinking moments, you must remember what happened to Peter:

"IMMEDIATELY JESUS STRETCHED FORTH HIS HAND, AND CAUGHT HIM."

MATTHEW 14:31, KJV

Where was the Lord?
WITHIN REACH.

Not on the shore shouting instructions or in the safety of the ship giving directions, He was in the water.
With Peter.
Reminding him not to doubt.

DON'T LET DOUBT KEEP YOU
FROM YOUR POTENTIAL.

WHEN THE LORD EXTENDS AN
invitation to act,
HE WILL NOT LEAD YOU INTO A
SITUATION THAT WILL DESTROY YOU.

He will reach your reaching.
He will be there to make sure you don't drown.
As the storm rages around you, He will speak of little
faith and remind you of the power of doubt.

HE WILL WHISPER WORDS
THAT INSTILL CONFIDENCE:

With me you are bigger than this.

Trust me.

Focus on me.

I know your potential.

AND THEN, HE WILL
CALM THE WIND.

"WELCOME THE TASK
THAT TAKES YOU
BEYOND YOURSELF."

—LOUISE YATES ROBISON

STEP INTO
THE WATER.

Peter had watched the Lord move through the crowd all afternoon—walking among the people with patience and compassion, teaching them many things, and healing those in need of healing.

It had been a good day.

A DAY FILLED WITH MIRACLES.

But now Peter was getting hungry, and he was exhausted.

He watched the Lord for a sign. Any time now the Lord would dismiss the crowd and the apostles would be able to sit down to eat and spend a quiet moment with Him.

It was what Peter was looking forward to most.

Finally, when the day was far spent, the Lord turned to His disciples.

"GIVE YE THEM TO EAT."

MARK 6:37, KJV

45

Peter was astonished by the Lord's request.

They were in the middle of a desert place. Obtaining food would require them to travel a long distance, and their purse did not contain the amount of money it would take to feed this multitude.

Besides, the time was far passed—they would never make it to the village and back before the sun went down.

He held out empty hands to the Lord and raised his shoulders in question.

The Lord's response confused him even more,

"HOW MANY LOAVES HAVE YE?"

MARK 6:38, ESV

The unexpected question came as a surprise.

The small group traveled with few provisions, and money was scarce. Even if they were to offer everything they had, it would not be enough. The obvious solution was to dismiss the multitude and allow them to return to the village to find food and shelter.

But this was not what the Lord had asked of them.

WHAT WAS IT HE WANTED THEM TO DO?

Peter looked at the Lord and again found that He was watching him intently. The look on His face was becoming familiar—expectation sparkled in His eyes, and Peter knew the Lord was about to extend an invitation that would require action.

WHAT DO YOU HAVE TO OFFER?

"GO AND SEE."

MARK 6:38, KJV

WHAT DID PETER DO?

WHAT WOULD

YOU

DO?

Peter gathered the disciples together to converse.

What did they have to offer?

What the Lord asked would require

SACRIFICE.

THEY WOULD HAVE TO GIVE

EVERYTHING THEY HAD.

It was Andrew, another disciple, who re-minded Peter about the young lad who carried a small basket containing what was to have been their supper.

They were not accustomed to fine meals.

This day, what little money they carried with them had been used to purchase the poorest of breads—five barley loaves. There had been enough left over to purchase two small, salted fish, commonly sold along the shores of Galilee.

It was hardly enough for them, and Andrew could not help but wonder, "What are they among so many?"

JOHN 6:9, KJV

PETER FELT A HINT OF RESERVATION
AS HE PLACED ALL HE HAD INTO
THE HANDS OF THE LORD.

The Lord gave thanks for the meager offering, broke it into pieces, and handed it to His disciples. They, in turn, gave it to the multitude, one by one, until each had received.

The abundance surprised Peter. There wasn't just one piece of bread and one piece of fish per person—the people ate until they were filled.

It was after the people had finished eating, after the twelve baskets were filled with what remained over and above, that Peter stopped to ponder.

He had given the Lord everything he had to offer.

Miraculously, the Lord had blessed it.

HE HAD MADE IT MORE.

The same event happened again some time later.

Another great multitude had gathered.

The question was familiar, "How many loaves do you have?"

MARK 8:5, NIV

The Lord didn't want to send the crowds away hungry.

SO HE FED THEM.

Once more there was enough and some to spare— seven baskets full to overflowing with bread. But somehow the disciples climbed into the ship without them. It was too late when they realized they had left them behind.

Now there was only one loaf to share between them, and one wouldn't be enough.

Hunger caused contention.

Before long the Lord responded, "Why are you talking about having no bread?"

MARK 8:17, NIV

"DO YE NOT REMEMBER?"

MARK 8:18, ESV

"WHEN I BROKE THE FIVE LOAVES
FOR THE FIVE THOUSAND,
HOW MANY BASKETS FULL
OF BROKEN PIECES
DID YOU TAKE UP?"

MARK 8:19, ESV

12

"And the seven for the four thousand, how many baskets full of broken pieces did you take up?"

MARK 8:20, ESV

7

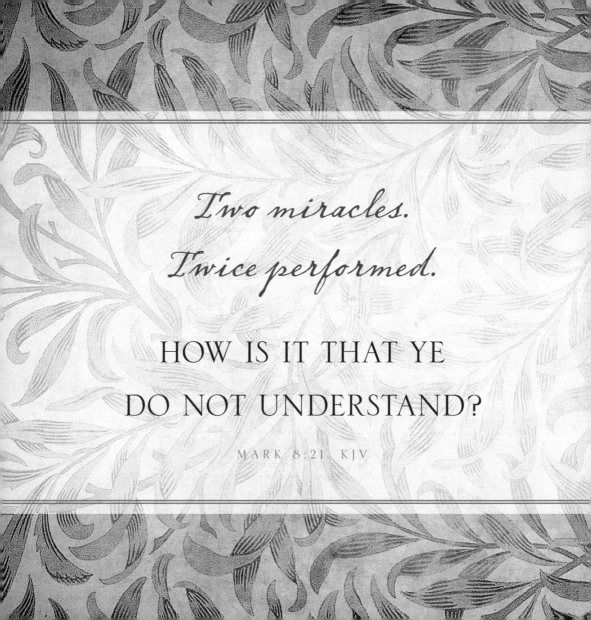

Two miracles.

Twice performed.

HOW IS IT THAT YE DO NOT UNDERSTAND?

MARK 8:21, KJV

"WE ALSO TOO OFTEN MISUNDERSTAND. SEEING THE SCANTY STORE IN OUR BASKET, OUR LITTLE FAITH IS BUSY WITH THOUGHTS ABOUT THE ONE LOAF, FORGETFUL THAT WHERE CHRIST IS, FAITH MAY EVER EXPECT ALL THAT IS NEEDFUL."

—ALFRED EDERSHEIM

It was only in their hands that the one loaf was lacking.

Why did they not remember what it could become in His?

ALL ALONG, THE LORD KNEW WHAT WOULD HAPPEN.

From the very first moment, when He asked the very first question, "How many loaves have ye?"

He said that to prove them, "for he himself knew what he would do."

JOHN 6:6, KJV

Here is an important truth: If the Lord knew what He was about to do in Peter's life, then He knows what He is about to do in *yours.*

You might feel like you are in a desert place.

It may seem as if the time for a miracle is far passed.

Perhaps you hold in your hands one single loaf, and you question if what you have to offer is *enough.*

WITH HIM, HOW COULD IT NOT BE?

DO YOU NOT REMEMBER?

How is it that ye do not
UNDERSTAND?

He knows *everything* about you. . . .

HE KNOWS what keeps you up at night

He knows what weighs on your heart

He knows your longing to become

something more.

If the Lord can do
GREAT THINGS
with a *single loaf*
imagine what He can do
with a *single life.*

The Lord is completely aware of you,
He has *miracles* in store for you,
and He knows what He is about to do.

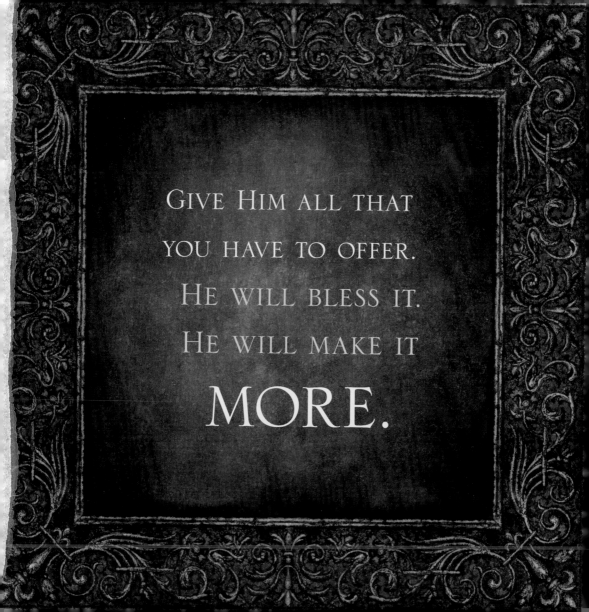

It was after the miracles had taken place.

After the walking on water and the multiplying of loaves.

The twelve apostles had come into the coasts of Caesarea Philippi. It was there that Jesus asked them a question . . .

"WHO DO YOU SAY I AM?"

MATTHEW 16:15, NLT

Why have *you* left wealth and reputation?

Why do *you* follow me?

Why are *you* living the lives that you are?

The Savior of the world, who knows the thoughts and intentions of every human heart, already knew the answer to the question He was asking that day.

WHY ASK A QUESTION YOU ALREADY KNOW THE ANSWER TO?

Peter looked intently at the Lord.

He saw a friend, a teacher, a mentor.

But there was more...

Nets once empty had become full.

The sea once furious had been calmed.

Peter had walked in places he would never have imagined.

Thousands had been fed from a few loaves.

Loaves that had been placed into His hands.

Lives that had been placed into His hands.

Hands that had power to do mighty things—

to change, to calm, to make something more.

Suddenly, the reason for the

question became *clear...*

Peter, who once thought himself just a fisherman, stepped forward and emptied his heart in a simple, powerful expression of faith.

"THOU ART THE CHRIST, THE SON OF THE LIVING GOD."

MATTHEW 16:16, KJV

In that moment, Peter left neutral ground, and in doing so, he put his heart into the hands of the Lord.

THERE WILL BE A POINT
IN THIS JOURNEY WHERE
YOU WILL HAVE TO
leave neutral ground.

THAT MOMENT WILL
REQUIRE YOU TO
GIVE HIM YOUR
HEART...
ALL OF IT.

HE IS THE CHRIST.

Let Him *guide* your life.

Counsel with Him.

Ask for His input.

Allow Him to *change* you.

Trust that He will make
you something *more*.

LEAVE NEUTRAL GROUND.

You should know that accepting this invitation will require you to take a stand.

Muster up *courage* for the journey ahead.

YOU ARE GOING TO NEED IT.

That night, the only light was the flickering of distant torches.

The gentle touch of the Lord's hand on his shoulder startled Peter and awoke him again. He lifted heavy eyelids and focused on the Lord.

"SIMON, SLEEPEST THOU?"

MARK 14:37, KJV

It wasn't that he wasn't willing—
it was that he was weak.

Almost as if it was a bad dream, he watched Judas approach the gate with a crowd of armed and angry men. In that moment, Peter realized he wasn't in the ship any longer—he was in the center of the fire.

WOULD HE SHRINK?

In the moment of inadequacy when the Lord asked if he could watch one hour.

SEE MARK 14:37

In the moment of fear when he lifted his sword in anger.

SEE JOHN 18:10

In the moment of doubt just before he heard the cock crow.

SEE MARK 14:71

WITH EVERY PASSING MINUTE, PETER FELT THE STRETCHING OF HIS SOUL.

"I WANT TO KNOW IF YOU WILL STAND IN THE *center of the fire* WITH ME AND NOT SHRINK BACK. . . . I WANT TO KNOW WHAT SUSTAINS YOU FROM THE INSIDE WHEN ALL ELSE FALLS AWAY."

—ORIAH MOUNTAIN DREAMER

Not every memory of a disciple is a fond one.

This very night Jesus had predicted that each of his disciples would be offended by him, that one of them would betray him and another deny him.

Peter, the great apostle, refuted the idea with conviction and fervor. "Lord, I am ready to go with you to prison and to death." LUKE 22:33, NIV

HOW FAR WOULD HIS DISCIPLESHIP GO?

Questions came from every side.

"Art not thou also one of this man's disciples?" JOHN 18:17, KJV

"Did not I see thee in the garden with him?"

JOHN 18:26, KJV

"Surely thou art one of them."

MARK 14:70, KJV

How would Peter answer?

How would

YOU

answer?

There are moments of decision we will each have to conquer.

Commitment must be tried in the fire.

Where is your breaking point?

What cost is too high?

Can you accept the Lord's invitations during bitter days when blessings seem so distant?

WILL YOU FORGET WHO YOU ARE MEANT TO BECOME?

It happened so unexpectedly.

The chanting of a hate-filled crowd,
"Crucify Him, Crucify Him!"

JOHN 19:6, NLT

The long walk up a dusty path to Golgotha.

SEE JOHN 19:17

The casting of lots, placing of nails, and lifting of cross.
The sword in His side. The wrapping of His
body with incense. The stone rolled in
front of the tomb.

SEE JOHN 19

AND THEN . . .

IT WAS OVER.

Surely Peter mourned.

He must have experienced the searching that deepens the soul.

Perhaps memories of failure lingered in his mind . . . the sleeping, the sword, the cock crowing.

In those moments, did he question whether the Lord really knew his potential, who he could become?

AND WHO WAS HE NOW, WITHOUT THE LORD?

After so many days of doubt, discouragement must have settled in.

But, on the third day,

hope returned.

It was Mary who came bearing the news, her eyes filled with fright and anticipation. He listened to her words—the stone rolled back, the linens folded, the tomb empty.

"THEN AROSE PETER, AND RAN UNTO THE SEPULCHRE..."

LUKE 24:12, KJV

His steps were driven by reckless abandon, his heart aflame with anticipation. There was no time to wait. The memory of the Lord's words haunted him, "Simon, sleepest thou?"

He had learned his lesson.

When given the opportunity to accept an invitation from the Lord, Peter would

COME RUNNING.

Heart pounding in his chest, he put one foot in front of the other until he was there.

"...AND STOOPING DOWN, HE BEHELD THE LINEN CLOTHES LAID BY THEMSELVES, AND DEPARTED, *wondering* IN HIMSELF AT THAT WHICH WAS COME TO PASS."

LUKE 24:12, KJV

"In moments of *wonder,*
it is easy to
avoid small thinking,
to entertain thoughts
that span the universe,

that *capture* both

thunder and tinkle,
thick and thin,
the near and the far."

—Yann Martel

Sometimes you have to set aside time for wondering.
You have to entertain thoughts of greatness.

In those moments, the Lord will
unfold possibilities
you have never even considered.

But every so often you may find yourself caught up in small thinking.

On those days, you might feel like it would be easier to go back to the way things were.

Peter must have.

Because, in the end, isn't that what he did?

HE WENT BACK TO WHAT HE KNEW BEST—FISHING.

Launch out into the deep

He was a simple fisherman on the shores of Galilee, but on that morning, Simon Peter was about to receive an invitation that would change the course of his life.

He had spent the whole night fishing with nothing to show for his labor.

When morning came, Peter lifted his gaze to the rising of the sun and saw a Man standing on the shore.

The Man called out a simple invitation, "Cast the net on the right side of the ship, and ye shall find."

JOHN 21:6, KJV

PETER KNEW THIS MOMENT.

He had experienced it before, three years earlier, in this same boat, with these same nets.

It happened in an instant—Peter cast the net on the right side, and they were not able to draw it in for the multitude of fishes.

As he reached over the side of the boat to grasp the net with his partners, his memory filled with images from that afternoon almost three years before:

The excitement and confusion, the gathering of fish and dividing of the load to make sure nothing was lost, the congratulations about his ingenuity and good fortune.

PETER GLANCED AGAIN TOWARD
THE MAN ON THE SHORE.

He knew the truth;
he recognized this invitation.

THE BOATS WERE SINKING
WITH *blessings.*

THE NETS WERE BREAKING
WITH *goodness.*

It didn't take long before the disciples recognized the miracle and began rowing to shore.

But not Peter.

When Simon Peter realized that it was the Lord, "he wrapped his outer garment around him . . . and jumped into the water."

JOHN 21:7. NIV

In his excitement to be with the Lord,

PETER JUMPED RIGHT INTO THE WATER AND BEGAN TO SWIM.

Step into the water

Peter pulled himself up out of the water. He wiped the sea from his eyes, shook his tousled hair back into place, and then turned to face the Lord. A warm fire of coals was waiting there.

FISH WERE COOKING.

AND BREAD.

LOAVES AND FISHES.

Miracles waiting.

BASKETS TO BE FILLED.

Give me all that you have to offer

The familiar twinkle lit up the Savior's eyes. "Bring of the fish which ye have now caught. Simon Peter went up, and drew the net to land full of great fishes, an hundred and fifty and three."

Then "Jesus saith to Simon Peter, Simon, son of Jonas, lovest thou me more than these?"
"Simon, son of Jonas, lovest thou me?"

"SIMON, SON OF JONAS, LOVEST THOU ME?"

JOHN 21:15, 16, 17, KJV

Leave behind your nets

How did Peter answer?

How would YOU?

Peter's eyes moved from the bursting net to the other disciples, then to the Lord.

Little did he know that the Savior was preparing to extend one last invitation.

An invitation that would include *two words*.

The same two words that had been spoken on this same shore three years before:

FOLLOW ME

Do you think anyone told Peter that he was destined for *remarkable things?*

That he was *extraordinary?*

That there was a *spark of greatness* in him?

THE LORD DID.

He told him who he *was*.

He showed him the *possibility*
of who he could *become*.

Without the Lord,
Peter was just a *simple fisherman*.

WITH THE LORD,
HIS *potential*
WAS IMMEASURABLE.

THE SAME IS TRUE FOR YOU.

There is a spark of greatness in you just waiting to be ignited. Your POSSIBILITIES span the universe. You have within you the POTENTIAL to become someone remarkable.

YOU WERE NOT SENT TO THIS EARTH
TO *play small* ...
TO *shrink* ...
TO *fail* ...

YOU WERE DESTINED TO
MAKE A DIFFERENCE.

YOU WERE MADE FOR
amazing things.

Accept His invitations...

LAUNCH OUT INTO THE DEEP

LEAVE BEHIND YOUR NETS

STEP INTO THE WATER

GIVE HIM ALL THAT YOU HAVE

LEAVE NEUTRAL GROUND

COME RUNNING

ENTERTAIN THOUGHTS
OF GREATNESS

EXPERIENCE *the* PETER POTENTIAL

Discover the life

YOU

were meant to live.

multiply
goodness

This book is meant to be shared.
We want you to give it away.
As you turned each page, did someone come to mind?
Someone you love.
Someone in need.
Could this message bring good into their life?
Then pass it along, and multiply goodness.

The world needs more good!
For more ways to share it,
visit www.multiplygoodness.com

IMAGE CREDITS

ABOUT THE AUTHORS

 *David Butler* is by day a high school religious educator sharing his love for the scriptures and his belief that there is a power for good innate in every human soul. By night he is a fort builder, waffle maker, sports coach, and storyteller for his five favorite little people, also known as his children. Somewhere in between he is a motivational speaker and writer. Some of his musings and challenges can be found on the blog www.multiply goodness.com. He and his wife, Jenny, live with their family amid the snow-capped peaks of the Mountain West, but they often dream of a beach house on a sunny shore somewhere.

 *Emily Belle Freeman* is a coach's wife, mother to four children and a few others who have found refuge in her home, author of several bestselling books, and sought-after inspirational speaker. Her days are spent watching over teenagers, her flock of pampered chickens, and a rabbit that she adores. She finds great joy in studying the life and teachings of Jesus Christ. Her deep love of the scriptures comes from a desire to find their application in everyday life. For a few minutes every day Emily forgets about the laundry, leaves the dishes in the sink, and writes. She coauthors a blog that is a stopping place for hearts seeking all that is good: www.multiplygoodness.com.